SEARCHING FOR YOU

ULRICH SCHAFFER

SEARCHING FOR YOU

TEXT AND PHOTOGRAPHY BY ULRICH SCHAFFER
CALLIGRAPHY BY FRIEDRICH PETER
PUBLISHED IN SAN FRANCISCO BY HARPER & ROW, PUBLISHERS
NEW YORK · HAGERSTOWN · SAN FRANCISCO · LONDON

FIRST EDITION

ISBN: 0-06-067083-5

LIBRARY OF CONGRESS CATALOG CARD NUMBER: 77-20458

FOR ALL THOSE
WHO ARE SEARCHING AND WAITING
AND WHO ARE NOT SATISFIED
WITH WHAT THEY HAVE

FOR ALL BEGGARS IN SPIRIT

COME
LET US SEARCH FOR HIM
HE IS WAITING TO BE FOUND

THE SILENCE RENEWS ME
AS I SINK INTO MYSELF
AND LOSE THE WEIGHT OF WORLDS
LIBERATED OF MY FEVERISH MIND
AND RELEASED FROM THE DRIVE
TO LIVE BY CALENDARS AND CLOCKS

IN THIS TIME AND SPACE
MY LIFE BECOMES VISIBLE AND AUDIBLE AGAIN
AND THE EVERYDAY BECOMES SIGNIFICANT:
THE WARMTH OF THE SUN MOVES THROUGH ME IN WAVES
I AM AGAIN TARGET TO THE RAINDROP
I AM HERE IN THE PRESENT

IN THIS SILENCE
I CAN TURN INTO A BIRD
AND SHOOT INTO THE BLUE
I BECOME LIGHT
AND SENSE THE WEIGHTLESSNESS OF ANOTHER WORLD
SO CLOSE TO THE ORIGIN
SO CLOSE TO YOU

MY EXPERIENCES WITH YOU
LOOM LARGE IN MY LIFE LORD
I FALL BACK ON THEM
I FEEL SECURE IN THEM

I CAN RECALL AND INTERPRET THEM
I LEARN THEIR MEANING
AND YET AGAIN AND AGAIN
THEY LEAVE ME EMPTY
BECAUSE THEY ARE PART OF YESTERDAY
WHICH IS GONE

I SEE THE NEWNESS OF THESE LEAVES BEFORE ME
NEVER BEFORE HAVE THEY BEEN GUESTS ON THIS TREE
THEY ARE THE PRODUCT OF SUNLIGHT AND EARTH
AND THEY PUT MY OLD LIFE TO SHAME
BECAUSE I AM NOT REBORN DAILY
IN THE NEARNESS TO YOU

I KNOW:
THAT WHICH IS GONE
IS GONE
YOU ARE HERE NOW
AND YOU WANT TO BE MY SUN AND MOON
LORD OF MY LIFE
IN THE BRIGHTNESS OF YOUR SUFFERING AND DEATH
YOU WANT TO RENEW YOURSELF IN ME
IN THE SUFFERING THAT I ACCEPT AS FROM YOU

NOW
YOU WANT TO BE MY LORD
UNCHANGEABLE AND CHANGED
BECAUSE I AM CHANGING
UNALTERED IN YOUR ABILITY
TO ADAPT TO MY LIFE AS MY STAR

THE WATER RUSHING AGAINST THE ROCK
SMASHING INTO PARTICLES OF LIGHT
REFLECTING THE INFINITE BLUE ABOVE
    TEACHES ME OF LIFE

THE GULL IN FLIGHT LIKE A SILENT STORM
FACING THE FIERCE NEEDLES OF THE WINTER WIND
PIERCED BY THE COLD PENETRATING ITS FEATHERS
    BANKS INTO MY LIFE
    AND TEACHES ME RESISTANCE

PRESSED TO THE GROUND INTO DEATH
SURROUNDED BY QUESTIONS LIKE SCAVENGERS
BROKEN-BONED AND BLINDED BY EMPTY SNOW
    I NOTICE YOUR LIFE TOUCHING MINE
    TEACHING ME OF YOUR SUFFERING
    FROM WHICH I AM REBORN ONCE AGAIN

YOUR GENTLE VOICE CALLS INTO MY SILENCE
SEARCHES ME OUT IN LOVE
OVERWHELMS ME WITH MANY FORMS OF LIGHT
AND I ANSWER YOUR CALL
WITH A HESITANT VOICE:
HERE I AM

I AM A SON OF GOD
A CHILD
THROUGH THE DEATH OF YOUR SON
I AM BLAMELESS AND PURE
IN THE GRACE THAT YOU HOLD IN READINESS
FOR ME

MY HEAD SWIMS
AT WHAT YOU HAVE DONE FOR ME
I DRINK IN THE LIGHT
THAT SPREADS OUT WITH YOUR PRESENCE
AND I AM WHOLE

I LONG FOR YOUR PRESENCE
I WANT TO TALK TO YOU
NOT ONLY IN PRAYERS
NOT ONLY IN THOUGHTS
I WANT TO SEE YOU
BUT NOT ONLY IN THE FACES OF OTHERS

I WANT TO TALK TO YOU DIRECTLY
I WANT TO SEE YOUR LIPS MOVE
TO SEE YOUR EYES LOOK INTO MINE
TO SEE YOU USE YOUR HANDS
TO SEE YOU SMILE
TO SEE YOU CRY

BUT YOU DON'T COME
AND MY LONGING REMAINS
NOW I WILL CONVERT THAT LONGING INTO ENERGY
AND THAT ENERGY INTO MAKING YOU VISIBLE
IN ME

FULL OF THE FEAR OF NOT KNOWING
AND NOT BEING KNOWN
NOT EVEN TO MYSELF
I RUN FROM EVERYONE
AND CONSTANTLY ARRIVE IN A SILENCE
BEFORE YOU
HUNTING THE ELUSIVE PEACE
THE FINAL RESTING IN YOU

FRIGHTENED OF SHADOWS
FRIGHTENED OF MY FEAR
    WHICH LOVE SHOULD HAVE CAST OUT
FRIGHTENED OF THE BRIGHTNESS OF THIS DAY
    BECAUSE OF ITS CONTRAST
    WITH ANY SUCCEEDING DARKNESS
AND FRIGHTENED OF YOU
I COME TO YOU

MANY FEELINGS FOR YOU AND THE WORLD AROUND ME
WAR WITH ONE ANOTHER IN ME
AND YET BEHIND ALL THOSE FEELINGS IS A CERTAINTY
THAT MY LIFE IS ROOTED IN YOU
WITH ALL ITS FEAR AND JOY
RESTLESSNESS AND AMAZEMENT
STRESS AND RELAXATION

AND ON THIS GROUND
I AM LEARNING TO MEET MY FEAR
TO MEET MYSELF

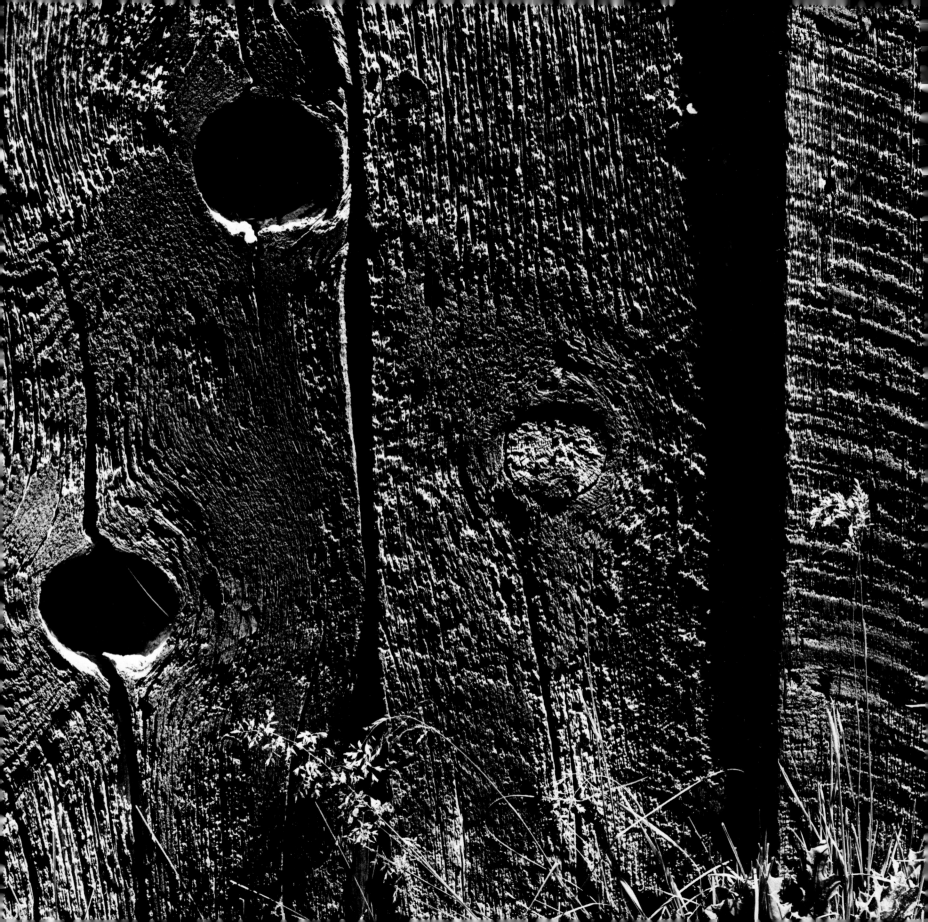

WHEN I WANT TO BE FREE AT ALL COSTS
I AM ALREADY BEGINNING TO BIND MYSELF
WHEN I PURSUE MY OWN WISHES
I THROW MYSELF IN CHAINS
I DO WHAT I DON'T WANT TO DO
I AM AT MY OWN MERCY

AND WHEN I FINALLY CONSIDER MYSELF FREE
FREEDOM BECOMES A BURDEN
BECAUSE I MUST MAKE DECISIONS
WHICH I AM UNABLE TO MAKE
AND MY FREEDOM TURNS INTO A NEW PRISON

I CAN ONLY FIND FREEDOM
IN THE ROPES THAT BIND ME
TO YOU

NEVER HAVE YOU GIVEN ME STONES
WHEN I HAVE ASKED
FOR THE NEARNESS OF YOUR SPIRIT
FOR THE BREAD OF MY LIFE

AND YET OFTEN MY HEART HAS BEEN STONE
I WAS HARD AND BLIND
FOR YOUR LOVE IN MY LIFE
AND WITHOUT THE PEACE OF YOUR DOVE

CHANGE MY BARREN LIFE INTO BREAD FOR THE WAITING
MAKE ME TRANSPARENT
AND TURN THE STONES INTO PEOPLE
ALIVE WITH THE FIRE OF YOUR SPIRIT

AN OLD SHIP'S HULL
IS DREAMING
OF GOLDEN TIMES
WHEN IT WAS
STILL PUTTING OUT TO SEA
WHEN IT COULD ROLL
IN THE BREAKWATER
AND TAKE THE WAVES
OVER ITS BOW
WITHOUT GOING DOWN

BUT I
WILL NOT DREAM
OF MY STRENGTH AND YOUTH
OF MISSED CHANCES
AND THINGS THAT WERE
AND WERE NOT

I WILL CALCULATE
THE LOW AND HIGH TIDES
AND PUT OUT ONCE MORE
INTO A TREACHEROUS SEA
FULL OF THE KNOWLEDGE
OF MY UNAGING CAPTAIN

THE GULL IS HEAVIER THAN AIR/ BUT BY ITS MOTION AND HOLLOW BONES
IT DEFIES GRAVITY AND RIDES THE WIND

IT IS THE MOTION OF FAITH/ AND THE KNOWLEDGE OF MY HOLLOWNESS
THAT ALLOW ME TO FLY AND BREAK THROUGH TO YOU

I AM HOLLOW BUT FILLED WITH HOPE/ AND THIS KNOWLEDGE MAKES ME LIGHT ENOUGH
TO SURVIVE THE STORM AND THE EYE OF THE STORM

TO BE HOLLOW AND TO KNOW IT/ IS TO BECOME FILLED WITH THE POWER TO FLY

I HAVE A STRONG YEARNING TO BE WITH YOU
MY LORD
IN THE HOPE OF PENETRATING
THE VEIL OF LIFE
TO DISSOLVE INTO LIGHT
THE DARKNESS OF MY LIFE
BECAUSE SO OFTEN I AM SEPARATED FROM YOU
BY THE BLINDNESS I HAVE FOR MYSELF

I YEARN TO BE CONSUMED
BY YOUR TENDER FIRE
TO BE DELIVERED INTO YOUR WISDOM
FROM MY DISTURBING IGNORANCE
TO BE PERMEATED BY YOUR WARMTH
AND FINALLY
TO BE MADE WHOLE
TO COME TO LIFE
BY YOUR DEATH
BRIGHTER THAN ANY LIFE
THAT EVER COMFORTED ME

I SENSE YOUR DRIVE
TO FLOW THROUGH ME
INTO THE SMALLEST BLOODVESSELS
BECAUSE YOU WANT TO BE MY HEARTBLOOD
IN ALL THE PASSAGES OF MY LIFE
AND YOU WANT TO BECOME VISIBLE IN THE LEAVES
AND THE FRUIT THAT I BEAR

SPREAD OUT IN ME
PRESS FORWARD PENETRATE PIERCE AND FLOW
EVEN IF AT TIMES
I WANT TO REPEAL THIS INVITATION
BEING AFRAID OF YOUR WAYS WITH ME

CIRCULATE IN ME
CHANGE AND RENEW
BECAUSE I KNOW
THAT ONLY YOUR SPIRIT
CAN BRING REAL LIFE AND FRUIT

WE WAIT IN OUR SLEEPING
WAIT IN SILENT STARING
FULL OF APPREHENSION
WE WAIT WITH SORROW AND REGRET
WITH A LEADEN HEAVINESS
THAT DOES NOT LET US FLY

BUT IN THE MIDDLE OF THIS HEAVINESS
I SEE YOU APPEARING
LEAST EXPECTED AT THIS MOMENT
MORE THAN A SHADOW
MORE THAN JUST THOUGHTS
AN OVERWHELMING PRESENCE OF NEW LIFE
A HOPE THAT KNOWS NO LIMITATIONS

YOU SET MY LIBERATION IN MOTION
YOU PENETRATE MY FEAR
AND WHEN I FEEL WEAK
YOU SHOW ME THAT IN MY WEAKNESS
YOUR STRENGTH LIES HIDDEN

SOMETIMES YOUR BRIGHTNESS
HITS ME LIKE A DARK CLOUD
AND I STOP KNOWING

I AM OVERCOME BY MY SHADOW
WHICH APPEARS IN ITS FULL DARKNESS
ONLY IN YOUR BRIGHT LIGHT

BECAUSE I HAD GROWN ACCUSTOMED TO MY TWILIGHT
I AM NOW LOST AS IN A FOG
AND I NOTICE FEAR SPREADING IN ME

I SHADE MY EYES AND MY LIFE
FROM YOUR LIGHT
TO REDUCE MY DARKNESS

BUT I KNOW I WILL BE OVERCOME
MY DARKNESS WILL BE TORN FROM ME
AND I WILL BE BATHED IN THE LIGHT OF YOUR DEATH

I WILL WALK STRAIGHT AND NOT CAST A SHADOW
BECAUSE I AM YOUR CHILD
MY FATHER

SUDDENLY
ONE MOMENT
THE WHOLE WORLD IS ABLAZE
AND I AM GIVEN THE VIEW THAT PENETRATES

IN THIS SECOND ALL LOOSE ENDS ARE TIED UP
EVERYTHING IS RIGHT
THE WORLD IS NO LONGER MADE OF PIECES
ALL QUESTIONS CEASE
BODY SOUL AND SPIRIT ARE NOT TORN APART ANYMORE

THE DOOR HAS BEEN PUSHED OPEN
THE VEIL IS GONE
AND THERE YOU ARE

I SENSE THE TRUTH
THAT LIES CONCEALED BEHIND THE IMAGES
THAT SETTLE ON MY RETINA

POWERFULLY
I AM DRAWN TO THAT WHICH HAS GROWN SLOWLY
AND DRIVEN ITS ROOTS DEEPLY
WHICH HAS PERMANENCE
AND KNOWS THE PAINS OF GROWTH

TO GROW IS MY WISH
BUT AM I PREPARED TO RECEIVE THE WOUNDS OF LIFE ?
TO LET ANY WEATHER PASS OVER ME ?
AM I READY TO GIVE SHELTER TO MANY
YET TO SEEK SHELTER ONLY WITH YOU ?

I WANT TO BE RADIANT FROM THE INSIDE
I WANT TO STAND FIRM AND TO MATURE
TO GROW INTO YOU
TO DRIVE MY ROOTS DEEPLY
TO LIVE THROUGH YOU
BUT I KNOW
THAT THE PRICE IS HIGH

AT TIMES I WANT TO CLOSE MYSELF OFF
SHUT EVERYONE OUT
AND ALLOW NO ONE TO LOOK IN
NOT EVEN YOU LORD
BECAUSE I HAVE TO HIDE THE VOIDS OF MY LIFE
THE EMPTINESSES THAT MAKE ME ASHAMED
AND UNCERTAIN OF YOUR REACTION

I WANT TO WITHDRAW
TO THINK AND WAIT
TO TAKE NO RISKS
NOT EVEN WITH YOU GOD
BECAUSE I WANT TO REMAIN IN CONTROL
OF MY LIFE

AS I HIDE AND DO NOT PRETEND TO BE OPEN
I NOTICE THAT I CAN AFFORD TO OPEN UP
THAT I CAN BE WHO I AM
AND STOP PLAYING A ROLE
THAT IN BECOMING TRANSPARENT TO MYSELF
I ALSO BECOME TRANSPARENT TO YOU AND THE WORLD

A WEIGHT IS TAKEN OFF ME
AND I FEEL THE WISH GROWING IN ME
TO LET YOU VIEW MY LIFE
THROUGH THE CRACKED AND PATCHED WINDOWS
THAT CAUSE ME LESS SHAME NOW

I WAIT OUT THE DARKNESS
THE FEELING OF NOT MATTERING TO MYSELF
TO OTHERS AND TO THE PASSAGE OF TIME

I LOSE ALL CONCERNS FOR MY IMAGE
ALL THOUGHTS OF EXPECTATIONS
ALL WELL-INTENTIONED AMBITIONS

THAT WAY I BECOME FREE TO BECOME MUCH LESS
THAN I APPEAR TO BE
IN ORDER TO BECOME MORE THAN I AM NOW

I SHALL USE THE DARKNESS AND TIME
TO BE TRANSFORMED INTO THE LIGHT
THAT YOU HAVE CHOSEN FOR ME

YOUR CHOICE FOR ME
IS MY GOOD FORTUNE

YOU ARE

I HEAR YOU
  IN THE CRY OF THE GULL
  IN THE WIND CHASING THE LAST LEAVES OF FALL
  IN THE WHISPER OF A CHILD
I SEE YOU
  IN THE ANIMAL SHAPES OF CUMULUS CLOUDS
  IN THE TREES TEN TIMES MY AGE
  IN THE WRINKLED FACE OF A WOMAN OVER NINETY
I TASTE YOU
  IN THE SWEETNESS OF WHOLE WHEAT IN BLACK BREAD
  IN THE SMOOTH RICHNESS OF AN AVOCADO
  IN THE CREEK WATER FROM A CUPPED HAND
I SMELL YOU
  IN THE AIR AFTER A CLEANSING RAIN
  IN THE FRESHLY CUT GREEN ONION
  IN THE THICK CARPET OF AUTUMN LEAVES

I TOUCH YOU
    IN THE SMOOTH BARK OF A WHITE BIRCH
    IN THE ROCK BENEATH THE SUMMIT TEARING MY HANDS
    IN THE TEXTURE OF WET AND DRY SAND

I READ YOUR LETTERS TO ME
    IN THE TALKING EYES OF A STUDENT
    IN THE JOY OF SHARED GRIEF
    IN THE NEW INNOCENCE OF A TEENAGER PRAISING YOUR NAME
    IN THE APPROPRIATE PHRASE RELEASING THE TENSION
    IN THE SILENCE THAT FOLLOWS THE STORM
    IN THE PLUNGE OF A SUICIDE
    IN THE NOVELIST CREATING HIS CHARACTERS
    IN THE TEAR CRIED IN SELF-PITY
    IN THE TELEPHONE THAT NEVER RINGS
    IN THE SHARP BARK OF A MACHINE GUN SOMEWHERE
    IN THE LIFE-CYCLE OF A SALMON
    IN THE NEWS THAT ENDS THE LIVES OF TEN THOUSAND
    IN THE CANDLE FLAME THAT DIES IN ITS OWN WAX
    IN THE WEIGHTLESSNESS OF A MAN WHO CAN'T CRY
    IN THE WHITE CANE OF A BLIND MAN
    IN THE EMPTYING CHURCHES
    IN THE BEGGAR'S MOUTH ORGAN
    IN THE UNFINISHED SYMPHONY
    AND THE UNPAINTED PICTURE

    LORD TEACH ME TO HEAR AND TO SEE
    TEACH ME TO TASTE TO SMELL AND TO TOUCH
    AND TEACH ME TO READ
    TO READ YOUR HANDWRITING
    YOUR LETTERS TO ME

LIFT ME UP
WHEN MY SHADOW WEIGHS ME DOWN
AND BLACKNESS MOVES IN FOR THE KILL

TEACH ME THAT MY FEAR
IS ONLY THE FEAR OF BEING AFRAID
AND THAT YOU ARE THE LORD OF THE FEAR

HELP ME TO TEAR MY EYES AWAY
FROM THE HYPNOTIC DETAIL
THAT STEALS MY OVERVIEW

AND FILL THE EMPTINESS
WITH YOUR EVIDENCE:
A SERENITY IN THE MIDST OF FEAR

BE MY CAPTAIN AND MY BOAT
MY OARS AND MY SAIL
AND THE WATER INTO WHICH I FALL

MY EYES ARE DRAWN UP TO A WORLD
THAT IS NOT YET MINE

WHEN MY GAZE COMES DOWN AGAIN
I STAND WITH FEET FIRMLY PLANTED
SOMETIMES ROOTED AND CHAINED TO BEDROCK

THAT IS MY DAILY EXPERIENCE:
DEATH AND CONSOLATION
LAUGHING AND CRYING
AND IN IT I LEARN TO RECOGNIZE
LIFE IN DEATH
AND DEATH IN LIFE

AND IN IT MY SPIRIT LOSES ITS NARROW LIMITS
STEEPED IN THE MIRACLE OF LIFE
YET BOUND TO THE DISCIPLINE OF SUFFERING

TEACH ME TO ENDURE THE TENSION
AND TO LIVE THE PRECISE NUMBER OF DAYS
THAT WILL CONSTITUTE YOUR FULLNESS

MY OUTSTRETCHED HANDS ARE BECOMING ACCUSTOMED
TO THE SOLITUDE INTO WHICH YOU HAVE THROWN ME
MORE ALONE
THAN I COULD EVER BEAR TO BE

I AM LEARNING TO LIVE
WITH THE DEATH YOU HAVE CHOSEN FOR ME
MORE PAINFUL THAN ANY DEATH
I HAVE EVER CHOSEN TO GO THROUGH

MY EYES ARE ADAPTING
TO THE DARKNESS YOU HAVE CHOSEN FOR ME
DARKER THAN ANY DARKNESS
I EVER KNEW AND CHOSE

I AM LEARNING TO RECOGNIZE
THE MANY DISGUISES OF YOUR LOVE
DEEPER THAN ANY LOVE
I HAVE EVER EXPERIENCED

AND SLOWLY IT DAWNS ON ME
BEING LONELY IS: TURNING TO YOU
DEATH IS: A DEEP AND JOYOUS LIFE
DARKNESS IS: FINALLY SEEING YOUR LIGHT
AND LOVE IS: BEING BORN OVER AND OVER AGAIN

YOU ARE
BREAD OF LIFE
WATER OF LIFE
PLACE OF LIFE
THOUGHT OF LIFE
MAN OF LIFE

MY DEATH AND MY LIFE
MY CROSS AND MY RELEASE
MY QUESTION AND MY ANSWER
CONTENT OF MY SEARCH AND OF MY FINDING
SIGN OF MY ACCEPTABILITY AND OF MY LONELINESS

SUN OF MY LIFE
TREE OF MY LIFE
PEARL OF MY LIFE
FRIEND OF MY LIFE
STRENGTH OF MY LIFE

THE SOIL OF MY BEING

WHEN I RESIST YOU
YOUR HAND BECOMES STRONGER IN MY LIFE

WHEN I SEPARATE MYSELF FROM YOU
YOU MOVE EVEN CLOSER

I CANNOT GET AWAY FROM YOU
BECAUSE YOUR BLOOD LIVES IN MY BLOOD
AS MY LIFE
AND YOUR DYING HAS BECOME MY HEART

I GET UP IN YOU AND COME ALIVE
IN YOU I AM RESURRECTED IN EVERY DYING

I SEE MY SOLITARY EXISTENCE
IN THE VASTNESS OF LIFE
AND I KNOW I WILL LEAVE HARDLY A MARK
ON THIS IMPRESSIONABLE PLANET

BUT I AM CONSCIOUS OF MY CONNECTION
TO THE INEXTINGUISHABLE BRILLIANCE
OF YOUR LIGHT FLOODING THROUGH ME
AND CHANGING EACH CELL IN MY BODY

AND AROUND ME I SEE OTHERS IN THEIR SOLITARINESS
OVERCOME BY THE SAME FORCE OF LIGHT
TRANSFORMED INTO NEW SELVES
AND VISIBLE TO EACH OTHER IN THEIR TRANSPARENCY

OH MY GOD
HOW BEAUTIFUL IS YOUR LIGHT

I LOOK INTO MYSELF
  ANXIOUS WHAT I MIGHT FIND
I DO NOT DISCOVER BEAUTY
  AND YET I AM BEAUTIFUL
I DO NOT FIND TRUTH
  AND YET I LIVE THE TRUTH
I FIND MUCH POVERTY
  AND YET I MAKE OTHERS RICH
I DON'T FIND PURITY
  AND YET MY TOUCH PURIFIES

THE MIRACLE IS:
HE IS IN ME
THE PERFECT ONE
THE PURE AND TRUTHFUL ONE

AND I AM NOT AFRAID ANYMORE
WHEN I SEE MY DARK SIDE
WHEN I BECOME DISAPPOINTED IN MYSELF
WHEN I DON'T ACHIEVE MY GOALS

MY PERFECTION IS FOUND IN HIM
AND HIS PERFECTION BECOMES VISIBLE IN ME

I OFTEN THINK OF FLEEING
THE IMPERFECTION OF THIS WORLD
THE DRYNESS OF THESE TIMES
IN FAVOUR OF LUSCIOUS GREENS

BUT I KNOW
THAT THE DROUGHT IS IN ME TOO
THAT IN ME THE WATER LEVEL IS SINKING
MY ROOTS CANNOT REACH IT ANY MORE
BRANCHES ARE DRYING OUT AND NEEDLES ARE FALLING
ONLY THE MOST ESSENTIAL CONTINUES TO LIVE
AND DRAINS THE RESERVES

I AM AMAZED
HOW LITTLE IS NECESSARY FOR SURVIVAL
HOPE ALONE IS ALREADY RAIN
AND WILL SUFFICE

.D BY THE DANDELION
GS OF THE UPDRIFT
NTO ENEMY COUNTRY

GROUND
N

BIRTH
NERATION OF FLYERS

SUDDENLY THE WHEEL OF MY LIFE STOPS
STILLNESS REPLACES MOTION
AND THE SOUNDS OF LIFE DISSAPPEAR INTO SILENCE

WITH FEAR I NOTICE THE STANDSTILL
BECAUSE I HAVE ALWAYS SEEN
GROWTH TOGETHER WITH MOTION
AND WISDOM TOGETHER WITH WORDS

UNREST AND APPREHENSION CREEP UP IN ME
I CRAVE FAMILIAR MOTIONS
AND PREDICTABLE WORDS

BUT THEN I NOTICE YOUR HANDS IN THE SPOKES
AND MY EYES ARE OPENED
TO THE LIFE PULSING THROUGH THE STILLNESS
AND MY EARS ARE OPENED
TO THE SILENCE ALIVE WITH YOU

RESTING CAN BE WORKING
MOTION CAN BE STANDSTILL
DISINTEGRATION IS OFTEN THE FIRST PHASE OF REBIRTH
AND THE DESERT IS IMMEASURABLY RICH IN LIFE
TO THE INNER EYE THAT SEES BEYOND
THE SAND AND THE SILENCE

THE WORLD AROUND ME POINTS TOWARD YOU
THE COUNTLESS LAKES OF THE NORTHERN LANDSCAPE
REFLECT YOU
THE BEAR GRUMBLES OF YOU
WHILE CATCHING SALMON FOR WINTERFAT
AND THE SPIDER THAT LOWERS ITSELF TO ME
WEAVES A WONDER IN DETAIL AND STRENGTH

BUT
YOU ARE NOT ONLY THE CREATOR
MIGHTY AND DISTANT
UNDEFINED AND NEBULOUS
YOU ARE MUCH MORE THAN SOME GOOD GOD
WHO MEANS WELL

YOU ARE ALSO MY BROTHER
WHEN YOU BECAME A MAN LIKE I AM
WHEN YOU STEPPED INTO MY LIFE BY YOUR DEATH
TO RELEASE ME TO A LIFE OF FULLNESS
TO BRING BACK YOUR CREATION
TO YOU

I AM AMAZED BY YOUR GREATNESS
AND YOUR NEARNESS
BY YOUR OMNIPOTENCE
AND YOUR INTEREST IN ME

YOU ARE BEHIND ME
I DO NOT HAVE TO TURN AROUND

YOU ARE IN FRONT OF ME
I AM WALKING TOWARD YOU

YOU ARE BESIDE ME
MORE THAN ANY ABYSS AND ANY MOUNTAIN

YOU ARE IN ME
I DO NOT HAVE TO LOOK ELSEWHERE

WITH YOU IN ME
I CAN FIND YOU EVERYWHERE

IN FRONT OF ME IS YOUR SIGNATURE
CARVED INTO A TABLET OF SANDSTONE
IT IS DECIPHERABLE BUT NOT EASILY TRANSLATABLE
INTO THE DAY TO DAY AFFAIR OF LIVING

THE SANDSTONE WILL CRUMBLE AND WASH TO THE SEA
BUT THE MESSAGE WILL BE WRITTEN
INTO THE BLOOD OF THOSE STRICKEN BY THE LAW
AND TOUCHED BY ITS FULFILLER

EVEN TODAY
WE CAN STILL HEAR YOU AS ON SINAI
AND WE CAN STILL SEE YOU ON THE CROSS
AT THE GOLGOTHA OF OUR LIVES

I AM CAUGHT IN MY OWN NET
I HAVE TRAPPED MYSELF
IN THE LIES OF MY LIFE
AND BEFORE ME IS DEATH

BUT
AS I AM BEING HAULED UP
THE KNOTS AND THE MESHWORK FADE
THE NET DISSOLVES AND FALLS AWAY
AS YOUR SUN BREAKS THROUGH

AND
I AM FREE
TO SWIM IN YOUR LIGHT

WHEN FOG ROLLS IN
ON DAYS THAT HAVE NO BEGINNING OR END
PUNCTUATED ONLY BY LONE BIRDCRIES
I FORGET WHAT THE SUN LOOKS LIKE
AS IT HIDES BEHIND DRIPPING DAMPNESS
AND ALLOWS MY LIFE TO BE WRAPPED IN FOG

BUT WHEN THE SUN BLEACHES
THE ALREADY DAZZLING BEACH
AND THE BEE BENDS THE FRAGILE FLOWER
IN A GRACEFUL ARC
I CANNOT BELIEVE THAT ANY FOG
CAN OBSCURE THE SUN EVEN FOR SECONDS

AND THEN I KNOW
THAT I MUST ENTER THE INVISIBLE
THAT I MUST GAIN THE INSIGHT OF THE BLIND MAN
THAT I MUST WALK WITHOUT LEGS
AND LEARN TO FLY BEYOND ANY SKY
TO SEE THE FOG IN THE SUN AND THE SUN IN THE FOG

COME AND BE MY TEACHER
HELP ME BREAK THROUGH TO THE CENTER
IN WHICH YOU APPEAR
AS THE HEART AND CORE

MY LIFE IS FULL OF APPREHENSION
AND I AM ENGAGED IN A STRUGGLE
THAT TAKES ALL ENERGY

SOMETIMES I AM JUST HANGING ON
IN SPITE OF MYSELF
LOOKING FOR SIGNS
AND HOPING FOR MIRACLES

I AM SURPRISED
THAT I AM
THAT I AM STILL HERE
IN THE MIDDLE OF LIFE

AND I BECOME AWARE OF GRACE

WHEN I FACE MY SOLITUDE
I BECOME RICHER
AS ALL WEIGHTS FALL AWAY FROM ME
AND I FIND PEACE

THE EMPTY SPACES
CONVEY YOUR PRESENCE
AND YOU BEGIN TO TALK MORE AUDIBLY
THAN THROUGH THE WISDOM OF MEN

I SINK INTO MYSELF
TO MEET YOUR GENTLE WIND
A TENT TO MY SPIRIT
AND A HOME FOR MY BROKENNESS

I SENSE YOUR TENDERNESS TOWARD ME
YOUR STRONG GENTLENESS
WHICH CONVINCES ME OF YOUR LOVE

I FEEL YOUR WISH FOR COMMUNION WITH ME
YOUR DESIRE FOR CLOSENESS
TO YOUR CHILD

I AM AWARE OF YOUR NEED FOR ME
BECAUSE I AM YOUR CREATION
ON THE WAY BACK TO MY CREATOR

I KNOW THAT I HAVE ALREADY BEGUN
TO FLOW INTO YOU
LIKE A RIVER INTO THE OCEAN

SOMETIMES I FEEL
THAT THE SILENCES SEPARATING MY POEMS
WHEN I HAVE LOST ALL DESIRE TO SPEAK
EVEN OF YOU
ARE THE GREATEST PRAISE I CAN OFFER YOU
AND THE MOST ARTICULATE SPEECH
I CAN HAVE FOR MY FRIENDS

IN THIS SILENCE I DELIVER MYSELF TO YOU
I REALIZE MY OWN INABILITY
MEET YOU EMPTY-HANDED
AND THROW MYSELF ONTO YOUR GRACE

PRESERVE THIS SILENCE
RICH WITH YOU
BURSTING WITH A DEPTH
THAT ALLOWS ME TO SEE
INTO THE HEART OF LIFE

LORD
HOW POOR I AM IN WINTER
WHEN I STOP GROWING
AND ONLY WANT TO SURVIVE

UNDER THE BURDEN OF SNOW
AND IN MERCILESS FROST
I CAN ONLY HOLD ON
TO THE HOPE OF SPRING

STAY WITH ME
AND PERFORM THE MIRACLE AGAIN:
LET THE GRIP OF WINTER BE BROKEN
COMPLETE THE CYCLE
AND LET ME BLOOM
AND BEAR FRUIT
ONCE MORE

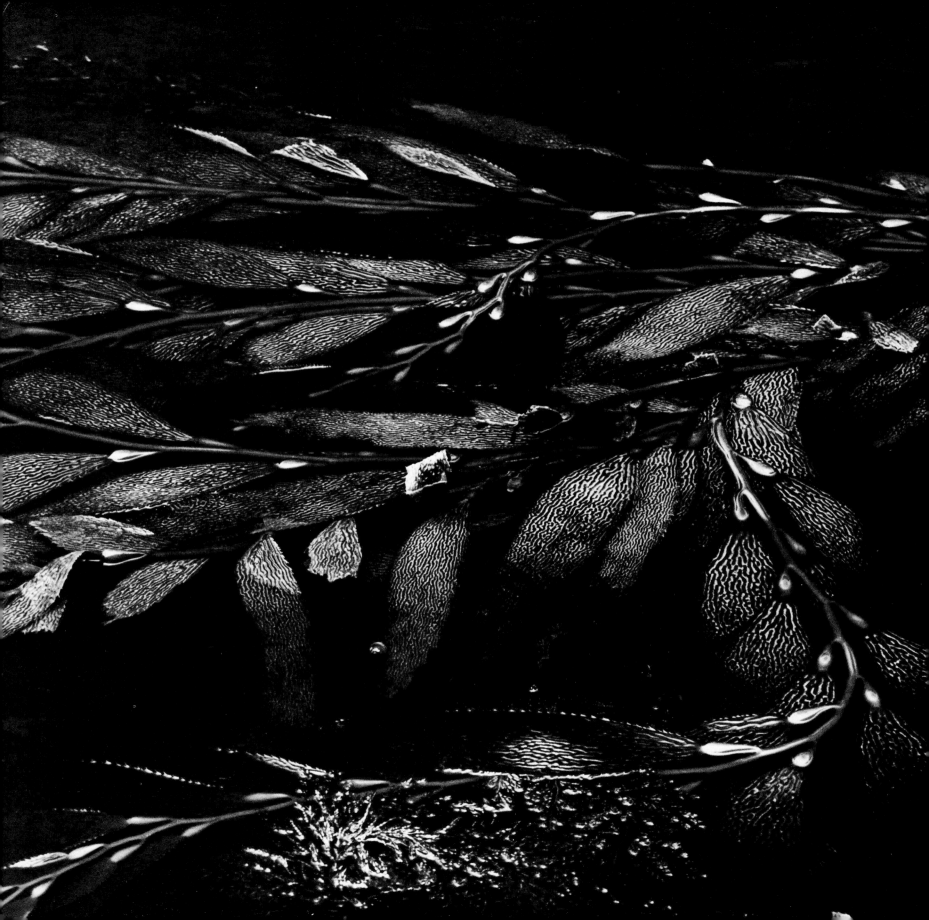

THE DEEP IS OPENING UP UNDER ME
I AM SWALLOWED BY THE SEA
AND I DON'T KNOW
HOW I CAN PREVENT MY DROWNING

THE WORLD AROUND ME COLLAPSES
NOTHING MAKES SENSE
ALL ACTIONS BECOME EMPTY
AND I AM SEARCHING FOR FIRM GROUND

THE WATER STANDS BETWEEN MY MOUTH AND NOSE
AND THE SUCTION OF THE ABYSS INCREASES

BUT THEN YOU INTERVENE
AND COME BETWEEN THE ABYSS AND ME
AND I AM HELD BY THE HAND
THAT I COULD NOT SEE BEFORE

NOW THE WATER LOSES ITS THREAT
AND I CAN FEEL LIKE A FISH
IN THE ELEMENT THAT CAUSED ME FEAR
BEFORE I KNEW OF YOUR HAND

IN EVERY ABYSS

YOU CARE FOR THESE STARLINGS
YOU SEND THEM TO SOUTHERN REGIONS
AND LET THEM RETURN IN TIME FOR THE CHERRY HARVEST

YOU LET THEIR YOUNG HATCH AT THE RIGHT TIME
AND YOU SUPPLY THE PARENTS WITH FLIES AND WORMS
TO STUFF THE BEAKS OF THE SMALL ONES
UNTIL THEY CAN FLY AND HUNT ALONE

WHY THEN AM I WORRYING ?
AM I NOT MORE THAN THESE STARLINGS ?
DID YOU NOT DIE FOR ME ?
DO YOU NOT LIVE FOR ME ?

I WILL TRUST YOU
AND NOT WORRY ANY MORE
I WILL BELIEVE
THAT I AM IN YOUR HAND

LIKE THESE STARLINGS

SOMETIMES THE CRY OF THE GULL
IS LIKE MY CRY
A CRY THROWN INTO THE GRAY SKY
DROWNED IN THE BATTERING SEA
WHICH CHANGES TO SAND
EVEN THE HARDEST OF ROCKS

A CRY PRESSED OUT BY THE FORCE OF LIFE
WHIPPED UP INTO AN UNFEELING UNIVERSE
A CRY IN YOUR DIRECTION MY FATHER
THE ONLY DIRECTION OF SENSE
THE ONLY RECEIVER

AND THEN I AM AFRAID
THAT MY CRY WILL ECHO BACK
AND COME CRASHING OVER ME
MAGNIFIED A THOUSAND TIMES
DEVASTATING MY LIFE IN A CYCLONE OF FRENZY
BECAUSE YOU HAVE NOT HEARD

BUT THEN THE SILENCE IN THE DEAD OF NIGHT
IS FILLED
AND THE VOID AT THE CENTER OF THE HEART
TURNS INTO A CELEBRATION
AT YOUR NEARNESS

AND I KNOW THAT YOU HAVE HEARD MY CRY

Regarding This Book

I am especially pleased, after four years of enthusiastic work on both the photos and texts, to be able to combine word and image in one book. Some may find the result too concerned with inwardness because it does not discuss social problems at all. I decided very consciously to go in that direction. Both photos and texts are to lead the reader and viewer into silence, and to the inner space of communication with God. I hope this will not be confused with a sentimental turning away from the world or a fearful fleeing from life.

Silence has become increasingly important to me in the last few years, and this book is a record of that development. I can only meet people meaningfully if I come out silence. Therefore, silence is an important part of my private, but also of my public, faith. In silence, in being alone, I prepare myself for interpersonal involvement. When I look at my relationship to God, I am at the same time looking at the central questions of life: questions of work and marriage, of poverty, of urban life, and of social injustice. Wherever I devote myself honestly to the questions touched upon in this book, there I will also gain a better perspective for the other questions of living. In short: my relationship to the world depends on my relationship to God! For this reason I dared to dedicate a whole book to looking inward. With this in mind I wrote the texts and selected the photographs.

This book is an expression of my personal experience and should be seen as such. I have tried not merely to theorize or intellectualize, because I am convinced that wherever we report genuinely and directly on ourselves we will create a bridge to others. In the last analysis our questions, joys, problems, and experiences are not that different from those of others. But we must not hide from each other. It is also important that each reader translate the statements of this book into his or her own life.

The texts were written between 1973 and 1977. I have chosen a more metaphorical language in contrast to my earlier books *(Love Reaches Out* and *A Growing Love),* and some might find these meditations more difficult to understand because of it. A language which is richer in images sometimes helps to penetrate more deeply into some of the important questions. Word images can open doors which might otherwise remain closed. In this light some texts should not be understood intellectually, but should rather be sensed or felt. The photos also stand in the service of digging more deeply. They were taken from 1963 to 1977 and are to aid the reader/viewer to enter into that silence or that interior space. I was therefore not so concerned with "beautiful" photos as with photos which could point beyond themselves, photos which could act as symbols and with which we could identify on a much deeper level. The photos were taken with different cameras, an assortment of lenses, and various films. In developing and printing I tend to prefer the harder grades of paper, which, at times, give some of my photos the character of an etching and at other times give more contrast because they eliminate almost all gray tones and single out fewer elements in the composition (see pages 30/31, 46/47, 78/79, and 88/89). But in spite of all the technical advances in photography and the almost unlimited possibilities, the most important factor in creating good photos is still the ability to see.

I would like to thank my friends who have helped me make the final selection of photos for this volume. A special thanks to Friedrich Peter who did the calligraphy and helped me with some of the technical matters. I would also like to thank my wife Traudi and my two daughters, Kira and Silya, for their patience when their husband and father seems always to be looking through the viewfinder of his camera when on a holiday, or to disappear into the darkroom for hours after returning from a holiday. A thanks also to those who appreciate books like this and thus enable people like me to create them.

Ulrich Schaffer
Burnaby,
British Columbia,
Canada
January 1978

Notes on the Photos and Texts

In these notes I would like to bring you into this book more by sharing my ideas that led to the finished product. I also mention some biblical passages which are related to the text on a given page.

Pages

7 *Photo:* Trees in fog on Burnaby Mountain, British Columbia, Canada, 1977.

8/9 *Photo:* Pacific coast in northern California, 1976.
Text: For fear of seeming too much like pantheists we usually do not dare to emphasize the omnipresence of God as I have in this meditation. "Be still and know that I am God" (Psalm 46:10).

10/11 *Photo:* Maple leaves behind our house, 1973.
Text: In Exodus 16 we are told that the Israelites only collected enough manna for that particular day. It could not be kept until the next day, because it went bad.

12/13 *Photo:* Rock in creek; North Vancouver, British Columbia, 1973. To me this rock is a symbol of strength, resistance, discipline, and persistence. I was especially fascinated by the light reflexes on the water to the right of the rock. It looks like the handwriting of water.
Text: The dynamic element for me is part of every rebirth. Being reborn is not a one-time happening on which we can rest. We have to strive to be transformed continually and to be changed by Christ. (See also p. 46.)

14/15 *Photo:* Light in the close-up of a dandelion (1973) and in a poplar tree in spring (1974).
Text: Hebrews 12:5-9; Revelation 21:7; Galatians 4:5. The perfection of the Christian is found in the death of Christ; Romans 8:1, 30, 33; Romans 10:10; 1 Corinthians 6:11; Colossians 2:10.

16/17 *Photo:* Grass on a dune in Oregon, 1976.
Text: Romans 8:22.

18/19 *Photo:* Wall of an old house in Bodie, California, 1976. Bodie is an old gold mining town which is now abandoned. I was intrigued by the texture of the wood and wanted to photograph it in such a way that one could feel the texture with his or her eyes.

20/21 *Photo:* Ropes, on the ferry from Vancouver to Vancouver Island, British Columbia, 1975.
Text: Romans 7:15; Romans 6:22; 2 Corinthians 3:7. "Where the Spirit of the Lord is, there is freedom."

22/23 *Photo:* Stones; Whiterock, British Columbia, 1974. The stones all seem to point toward the upper right hand corner.
Text: Luke 11:13; John 6:31-34; Acts 1:8; Matthew 3:11.

24/25 *left Photo:* Wreck; Third Beach, Vancouver, British Columbia, 1974. I was interested in the symbolism of this photo. The ship's wreck seems to dream while the other ship is anchored offshore. I have tried to capture that in the text. Dreaming is an important part of our life but it should not become a fleeing from life.
right Photo: Seagull, Vancouver, British Columbia, 1974.
Text: When we stop trusting solely ourselves and our capabilities then God can step in with his grace.

26/27 *Photo:* Woods in fog; Carmel, California, 1976.
Text: 1 Corinthians 13:12.

28/29 *Photo:* Leaf of a gunnera plant; Burnaby, British Columbia, 1975.
Text: "It is the spirit that gives life." John 6:63; 2 Corinthians 3:17.

30/31 *Photo:* Dock on the Elbe river in northern Germany, 1963.
Text: 2 Corinthians 12:9-10; Proverbs 10:28.

32/33 *Photo:* Marsh Landscape on the Elbe river in northern Germany, 1963.

34/35 *Photo:* Snowladen branches; Burnaby, British Columbia, 1975.

36/37 *Photo:* Old tree on Point Lobos near Carmel, California, 1976. The majesty combined with the sense of suffering in this tree caught my imagination. The shack under the tree is at the same time dwarfed and sheltered by it.
Text: Ephesians 4:15; Colossians 1:11.

38/39 *Photo:* Window in Bodie, California, 1976 (see also p. 19).
Text: Psalm 139:23.

40/41 *Photo:* Wreck Beach, Vancouver, British Columbia, 1965.

42/43 *Photo:* Siwash Rock, Vancouver, British Columbia, 1977. This rock is only a few yards offshore in the Pacific and it is joined to the mainland at low tide. The West Coast Indians developed legends about its origin.
Text: The first half of this meditation is concerned with becoming aware of God through our five senses. The second half goes beyond that and asks questions like: What can I learn from the happenings around me? What happens in me when I hear about a suicide or when I see a blind person? What does it all tell me about the world and myself? With God in my life I see the world differently than without him.

44/45 *Photo:* Aspens in the Cariboo, British Columbia, 1975.
Text: Romans 8:28 (see also the note to p. 43).

46/47 *Photo:* Near Blankenese on the Elbe river, northern Germany, 1963. I wanted to capture the almost perfect reflection.
Text: Psalm 139:2-3. God is sometimes seen as the captain of our lives. I found that too limiting and wanted to expand the image, and so God became even the water into which we fall: No one shall snatch us out of God's hand (John 10:28),

and nothing shall separate us from the love of God (Romans 8:35-39).

48/49 *Photo:* Aspens against the sky; Cariboo, British Columbia, 1974.
Text: There is always a discrepancy between what we can imagine and what we actually experience. St. Paul says in 2 Corinthians 5:7 "We walk by faith, not by sight." Or in 1 Corinthians 13:12 he says: "Now we see in a mirror dimly, but then face to face." Until that day, our life is in tension, but it is in just this tension that we mature.

50/51 *Photo:* Plant on a dune in Oregon, 1976.
Text: Psalm 71:20 (see also note to p. 14).

52/53 *Photo:* Field in northern Germany, 1977.
Text: John 6:35; Matthew 13:46.

54/55 *Photo:* Root on Hornby Island, British Columbia, 1977.
Text: I have tried to express the incredible love of God which pursues us wherever we are.

56/57 *Photo:* Solitary tree in the Devil's Moor near Worpswede in northern Germany, 1977.
Text: Our sense of being lost and alone in the world and the awareness of the nearness of God often lie so very close together.

58/59 *Photo:* Grasses with dew; Cariboo, British Columbia, 1977.
Text: Romans 8:1; Colossians 2:10; 1 John 1:7.

60/61 *Photo:* Dry Pines on Point Lobos near Carmel, California, 1976. In this photo I wanted to create a real sense of dryness.
Text: Romans 12:12; Hebrews 10:23.

62/63 *Photo:* Dandelion; British Columbia, 1975. The picture was taken from directly above. For that reason no stems can be seen and the grass appears as a very dark background.
Text: John 12:24. It is one of the most central statements of the message of Christ that life can only come about through death.

64/65 *Photo:* Hub of old wheel; Fort Steele, British Columbia, 1975. Fort Steele was one of the first forts of British Columbia.
Text: Much in the teachings of Jesus is conveyed in terms of paradoxes. "Many that are first will be last" (Matthew 19:30); Matthew 5:3-12; concerning the "resting" see Hebrews 4:9-11.

66/67 *Photo:* Spider web; Burnaby, British Columbia, 1976. To make the dew drops on the web more clearly visible I held some black cardboard behind it.
Text: Psalm 104; John 17.

68/69 *Photo:* Daisies; Burnaby, British Columbia, 1974.
Text: Luke 17:21.

70/71 *Photo:* Sandstone formations on Hornby Island, British Columbia, 1977. Through constant erosion this cliff face has the character of a tablet with a message.
Text: God touches us through the Law and through Love.

72/73 *Photo:* Fish nets; Steveston, British Columbia, 1974.
Text: Confessing and bringing our sins to the light activates God's grace (1 John 1:7-10). "But if we judged ourselves truly, we should not be judged" (1 Corinthians 11:31).

74/75 *Photo:* Foggy landscape near Carmel, California, 1976.
Text: 1 Samuel 16:7; Psalm 119:18.

76/77 *Photo:* Spotted Lake near Osoyoos, British Columbia, 1974. The alkaline deposits in this lake give it its interesting pattern. In the foreground is a dock. The photo was taken from a hill which explains the perspective.
Text: Psalm 22:12; Psalm 25:17; Psalm 103:11; Isaiah 54:10; 2 Corinthians 12:9; Titus 2:11.

78/79 *Photo:* Man in boat on the Elbe river, northern Germany, 1963.
Text: "gentle wind," see 1 Kings 19:11-13. For the wandering Israelites God made himself present in the tabernacle, a portable tent. See Exodus 25; Exodus 33:7-11; Deuteronomy 31:15.

80/81 *Photo:* Poppies against the light; Burnaby, British Columbia, 1973.
Text: God is wooing us. He does not force us but seeks our voluntary response (Matthew 11:29-30). Concerning the last stanza see Colossians 1:15-17.

82/83 *Photo:* Burnaby Mountain in fog, 1975.
Text: Silence has to be an integral part of our speaking, otherwise speaking will be just chattering. Psalm 46:11; Psalm 65:2; Isaiah 30:15; 1 Thessalonians 4:11.

84/85 *Photo:* Tree in winter; Mt. Seymour, near Vancouver, 1974.
Text: John 15:5-8; Galatians 5:22.

86/87 *Photo:* Kelp off the coast of Point Lobos, California, 1976.
Text: Psalm 61:2-3; John 16, 33; John 10:28.

88/89 *Photo:* Starlings; Steveston, British Columbia, 1974.
Text: Psalm 104:27-29; Matthew 10:29-31; John 4:34.

90/91 *Photo:* Rock in the surf; northern California coast, 1976. A small aperture and a fast shutter speed allowed me to shoot directly into the sun. The rock has something archetypal to it. It is a symbol of refuge but also of protest.
Text: Jeremiah 33:3; Joel 3:5.